Mind Traps

Unraveling the Labyrinth of Cognitive Biases and Heuristics

Freudian Trips

Copyright Page

Disclaimer

The views and opinions expressed in this book are those of the author(s) and do not necessarily reflect the official policy or position of any other agency, organization, employer, or company. The contents of this book are for informational and educational purposes only and are not intended to serve as professional advice, diagnosis, or treatment.

The information provided in this book is believed to be accurate and reliable as of the date of publication. However, it may include some errors or inaccuracies, and no warranty or guarantee is provided regarding the accuracy, timeliness, or applicability of the content.

Readers are encouraged to consult with professional philosophers, educators, or other qualified professionals where appropriate for personalized advice. The author(s) and publisher shall not be liable for any loss, damage, or harm caused or alleged to be caused, directly or indirectly, by the information or ideas contained, suggested, or referenced in this book.

By reading this book, the reader acknowledges and agrees that they are solely responsible for how they interpret and apply the information contained herein.

This book may also include references to other works, studies, and sources. These references are provided for further reading and exploration and do not imply endorsement or validation of the specific theories, viewpoints, or interpretations presented in those works.

Chapter 1: Introduction – The Invisible Influencers of Our Minds

Welcome to the World of Cognitive Biases and Heuristics:

Imagine walking through a dense forest, where every turn you take is influenced subtly by the paths that have been trodden before. This is similar to how our minds work when making decisions. We often think we're making entirely rational choices, but in reality, our thoughts and decisions are shaped by hidden forces known as cognitive biases and heuristics.

Cognitive Biases: The Hidden Tendencies of Our Minds

Cognitive biases are like invisible lenses that slightly distort how we see the world. These are the tiny mental idiosyncrasies that can cause us to make illogical or non-rational conclusions. For instance, have you ever bought something just because it's on sale, even if you didn't need it? That's a cognitive bias in action – we overvalue the satisfaction of getting a deal, even when it's not the best choice.

Heuristics: Mental Shortcuts in Our Daily Lives

Heuristics, on the other hand, are like mental shortcuts. They help us make decisions quickly without having to stop and think about every little detail. For example, if you're trying to choose the best route to work, you might pick the one you always take, not because it's the fastest, but because it's familiar. Heuristics are helpful, but sometimes they can lead us astray.

Why Does This Matter?

Understanding these mental patterns is crucial. They influence everything from our daily choices to major life decisions, and they can impact our relationships, work, and happiness. By learning about them, we can start to recognize these patterns in ourselves and others, and maybe even make better, more informed choices.

A Brief Stroll Through History

The study of cognitive biases and heuristics isn't new. In fact, it's a fascinating journey through time. It began in earnest in the 1970s with two psychologists, Daniel Kahneman and Amos Tversky, who started to uncover the systematic ways in which our decision-making deviates from what we would expect if we were entirely logical. Their work opened the door to a whole new understanding of the human mind.

Ready for the Adventure?

As we embark on this journey together, we'll explore the myriad ways our thinking is influenced by these hidden forces. We'll uncover the surprising and sometimes amusing ways our minds work. Most importantly, we'll learn how to navigate the labyrinth of our cognitive biases and heuristics, armed with knowledge and understanding.

So, let's step into the intriguing world of our own minds, shall we? It's time to discover the unseen influences that shape our thoughts, beliefs, and decisions every day. Welcome aboard!

Chapter 2: The Framework of Thought – Decoding Our Mind's Patterns

Unraveling the Mystery of Cognitive Biases

Have you ever wondered why you tend to favor the first piece of advice you hear over others that come later? Or why you instinctively like people who remind you of someone you already know? These are examples of cognitive biases at play. Simply put, cognitive biases are like mental shortcuts or filters that our brains use to simplify the processing of the vast amount of information we encounter daily. They can shape our perceptions, influence our decisions, and sometimes, lead us astray from logical thinking.

Cognitive Biases vs. Heuristics: What's the Difference?

Think of cognitive biases as the 'why' behind our irrational choices and heuristics as the 'how' we make quick decisions. Biases often involve an emotional or moral judgment, leading us to make choices based on our preferences or beliefs rather than facts. For instance, if you always buy the same brand of cereal, not because it's necessarily the best, but because it's familiar, that's a bias.

Heuristics, on the other hand, are like mental rule-of-thumb strategies we use for problem-solving when we don't have all the time or information. Imagine you're trying to guess the number of jellybeans in a jar. You might base your guess on the size of the jar or compare it to a similar jar you've seen before. That's a heuristic in action – a practical method to arrive at a decision quickly, but not always accurately.

The Brain's Role in Crafting Our Biases

Our brains are incredibly powerful, but they have their limits. To manage the sheer volume of information and decisions we face every day, our brains develop these biases and heuristics. It's like having a personal assistant in your head, trying to streamline the work by taking shortcuts. But, just like an overworked assistant, sometimes the brain takes shortcuts that aren't perfect, leading to biases.

These biases are not just random. They are shaped by various factors – our past experiences, cultural norms, emotional states, and even the way information is presented to us. For example, if you grow up hearing that cats are sneaky, you might develop a bias against them, even if you've never met a cat that was sneaky!

Why This Matters to You

Understanding cognitive biases and heuristics is like learning the rules of a game – it helps you play better. In life, this means making decisions that are more informed, fair, and objective. It also means you can understand others better, knowing that their decisions are also influenced by these hidden mental patterns.

Chapter 3: A Catalog of Biases - Navigating the Maze of Our Mind

Welcome to the World of Cognitive Biases

Imagine your mind as a vast, bustling city. Just as cities have shortcuts and well-trodden paths, our minds have cognitive biases - predictable patterns of thought that sometimes lead us astray. This chapter is like a guided tour of this city, showing you some common 'streets' (biases) and how they influence our daily lives.

1. Confirmation Bias: Seeing What We Want to See

Have you ever had a hunch about something and then looked for information to back it up? That's confirmation bias in action. Our inclination is to pay attention to data that supports our preexisting opinions and disregard that which doesn't. Think about the last time you wanted to buy a certain type of car and suddenly started seeing it everywhere. That's not because there are more of them around; it's because you're more tuned in to noticing them.

Real-World Example: In the stock market, investors often fall for confirmation bias by paying attention only to financial analysis that supports their preferred stocks while ignoring contrary evidence.

2. Anchoring Bias: The First Thing Sticks

Anchoring bias happens when we rely too heavily on the first piece of information we receive. Imagine going to buy a TV and the first one you see is priced at $1000. As you look at other TVs, you might think $850 is a good deal, even if $850 is above your intended budget. That initial $1000 price tag is your 'anchor'.

Real-World Example: In salary negotiations, the first number mentioned often sets the tone for the rest of the discussion, influencing the final agreed-upon salary.

3. Hindsight Bias: The "I Knew It All Along" Feeling

Ever watched a mystery movie and thought, "I knew who the culprit was!" after the reveal? That's hindsight bias. It's our tendency to see events as having been predictable, even though they weren't. This bias can lead us to oversimplify past events and believe we understand them better than we actually do.

Real-World Example: After a team loses a big game, fans and commentators might say the loss was obvious due to certain factors, even though it wasn't predictable before the game.

4. Availability Heuristic: What Comes to Mind Easily

The availability heuristic is about judging the frequency or probability of something based on how easily examples come to mind. For instance, if you watch a lot of news about airplane accidents, you might overestimate how risky flying is, even though air travel is statistically much safer than driving.

Real-World Example: People often overestimate the likelihood of dramatic or sensational events (like shark attacks or lottery wins) because these events are more memorable and get more media coverage.

And Many More...

There are numerous other biases – from the overconfidence bias, where we overestimate our own abilities, to the bandwagon effect, where we do something just because everyone else is doing it. Each of these biases is like a different street in the city of our minds, leading us in various directions.

Conclusion: Why This Matters

Understanding these biases is like having a map of the city. It helps us navigate better, make more informed decisions, and understand the decisions of others. As we go through life, being aware of these biases can help us pause and consider whether we're thinking clearly or just following a familiar but potentially misleading path.

In the next part of our journey, we'll explore each of these biases in more detail, uncovering the fascinating ways they shape our perceptions, decisions, and interactions with the world. Let's continue to explore the intriguing pathways of our minds!

Chapter 4: The Heuristics That Guide Us - Navigating Life's Shortcuts

Understanding Heuristics: The Brain's Quick-Decision Makers

Imagine you're late for an appointment and need to choose the fastest route. You don't have time to consider every possible road, so you quickly choose the one you usually take. There's a heuristic at play here. Heuristics are mental short cuts that allow our brains to decide quickly without needing to consider every little detail. They're like the brain's version of 'autopilot' for everyday decision-making.

Common Types of Heuristics

Representativeness Heuristic: Judging by Similarity

Imagine you meet someone who is quiet and loves reading. You might quickly assume they're an introvert, based on the similarity of these traits to your idea of an introverted person. This is representativeness heuristic, where we judge the probability of something based on how much it resembles a typical case.

Availability Heuristic: What Comes to Mind Easily

This is about estimating the likelihood of events based on how easily examples come to mind. If you frequently hear news about plane crashes, you might overestimate the risks of flying, simply because those incidents are more memorable.

Anchoring Heuristic: The First Thing You Hear Sticks

This is when we rely heavily on the first piece of information we get. For example, if you first see a sweater priced at $100, and then find a similar one for $70, you might feel like you're getting a great deal, even if you initially intended to spend only $50.

The Double-Edged Sword of Heuristics

Heuristics are incredibly useful. They help us make swift decisions in a complex world. Without them, we'd be overwhelmed by the minutiae of daily choices. However, these shortcuts can also lead us to make inaccurate or biased judgments.

For instance, while the representativeness heuristic helps us make quick assessments, it can also lead to stereotypes. Similarly, the availability heuristic makes us prone to overestimating the likelihood of dramatic events, which can fuel unnecessary fears.

Why This Matters to You

Understanding heuristics empowers you to recognize when you're using these mental shortcuts and to question whether they're leading you to the best decision. It also helps in understanding why others might make certain decisions that seem illogical at first glance.

In Summary

As we journey through life, being aware of these heuristics is like having a map and a compass; they guide us in making faster decisions but also remind us to occasionally stop and ensure we're heading in the right direction. In the next section, we'll explore more about how these heuristics influence our daily lives and decision-making processes, shedding light on the fascinating workings of our minds. Let's continue to navigate the shortcuts of our thinking together!

Chapter 5: Biases in Action - How Our Hidden Judgments Shape Our World

The Invisible Forces Behind Our Choices

In this chapter, we explore how the subtle, often unnoticed biases and heuristics we've discussed impact our daily decisions and judgments. It's like uncovering the invisible puppet strings that influence our every move.

How Biases and Heuristics Influence Our Decisions

In Our Personal Lives

Imagine you're choosing a new car. You might think you're basing your choice on facts like fuel efficiency or price. But often, biases like brand loyalty (a type of confirmation bias) or the influence of a friend's choice (social proof bias) play a significant role. Similarly, when meeting new people, first impressions can create an anchoring bias that affects how you perceive them long-term.

In the Professional World

In business, leaders often face the challenge of decision-making under pressure. The availability heuristic might lead them to make decisions based on recent events rather than a thorough analysis. Or, confirmation bias might cause them to favor information that supports their existing views, overlooking critical counterpoints.

Real-World Examples: Biases and Heuristics at Play

Business Case Study: The Tech Industry

Consider a tech company deciding to develop a new product. If the decision-makers rely too heavily on their success in past projects (overconfidence bias), they might underestimate the challenges, leading to overbudgeting and delays.

Political Scenario: Election Campaigns

Politicians often use heuristics to sway public opinion. For example, by highlighting specific incidents (availability heuristic), they can make certain issues seem more prevalent, influencing voter opinions and decisions.

Personal Relationships: Family Dynamics

In families, hindsight bias can lead to misunderstandings. For instance, after an argument, one might think, "I knew this was going to happen," even though it wasn't predictable, thus oversimplifying complex family dynamics.

The Impact on Our Lives

The influence of biases and heuristics extends to nearly every facet of our lives. In personal relationships, they can color our perceptions and interactions. In the workplace, they can shape leadership and decision-making processes. Even in our societal and political views, biases play a crucial role.

Why Understanding This Matters

By being aware of these biases and heuristics, we can start to recognize and mitigate their impact. This awareness allows us to make more balanced, informed decisions and understand the decisions of others with more empathy and clarity.

Conclusion: Navigating the Waters of Decision-Making

As we conclude this chapter, think of understanding biases and heuristics as a tool, much like a compass, guiding you through the complex journey of decision-making and judgment. By being aware of these subtle influencers, we can aim to navigate our personal, professional, and societal worlds with greater understanding and less hidden influence.

Chapter 6: The Social Dimension of Biases - How Our Surroundings Shape Our Thoughts

The Influence of Others on Our Decisions

Have you ever agreed with a group's decision even when you secretly disagreed? Or noticed that your opinions are sometimes swayed by the culture you're part of? In this chapter, we delve into how our social environments, including groups, culture, media, and technology, influence our cognitive biases and heuristics.

1. Groupthink: When Harmony Trumps Decision Quality

Groupthink is a phenomena that happens when decisions are made in an illogical or dysfunctional way because of a desire for group harmony or uniformity. It's like going with the flow, even when the river might be leading you in the wrong direction.

Example in Action: Imagine a team at work where everyone seems to agree on a flawed plan because no one wants to rock the boat. This can lead to missed opportunities or even major blunders because critical thinking is set aside for the sake of group unity.

2. Cultural Influences: The Lens of Our Environment

Our cultural background can significantly influence our biases and heuristics. The values, beliefs, and norms of our culture can shape how we see the world, often in ways we're not even aware of.

Example in Action: In individualistic cultures, there might be a stronger bias towards attributing success to personal effort (self-serving bias), while in more collectivist cultures, success might be more often seen as the result of group effort and external factors.

3. Media and Technology: Amplifiers of Biases

In today's digital age, media and technology play a huge role in shaping and reinforcing our biases. From the news we read to the social media algorithms that decide what we see, technology can both expose us to a wider world and trap us in echo chambers.

Example in Action: Social media platforms often show us content that aligns with our existing beliefs, strengthening our confirmation biases. This can create a feedback loop where our views become more extreme, as we're not exposed to differing perspectives.

The Ripple Effect in Our Lives

These social dimensions of biases can have profound effects on everything from our personal relationships to our societal structures. Groupthink can lead to poor decision-making in organizations, cultural biases can affect how we interact with people from different backgrounds, and media-driven biases can influence our opinions and actions.

Why This Matters

Understanding the social dimensions of biases helps us see the bigger picture - that our thoughts and decisions are not just shaped by our own minds but also by the world around us. It encourages us to seek diverse perspectives, question the status quo, and be more critical of the information we consume.

Conclusion: Navigating the Social Labyrinth

As we wrap up this chapter, think of yourself as a navigator, steering through the complex social waters of biases and heuristics. By being aware of these influences, we can strive for more informed, balanced, and empathetic viewpoints, both as individuals and as a society.

In the next chapter, we will explore strategies to counteract these biases, empowering us to think more independently and make decisions that are more reflective of our true selves and the diverse world we live in. Let's continue to uncover and understand the unseen forces that shape our social interactions and decisions.

Chapter 7: Overcoming Our Inherent Biases - Charting a Clearer Course

Unlocking the Chains of Unconscious Bias

We all have biases, but the good news is that we're not helpless against them. This chapter is about breaking free from the invisible chains of our inherent biases by learning to recognize, understand, and counteract them.

1. Strategies for Recognizing Biases

The first step in overcoming biases is to recognize that we have them. It's like turning on a light in a room that's always been dark. Here are some strategies:

Self-Reflection: Regularly take time to reflect on your decisions. Ask yourself, "Why did I make that choice? Was I influenced by a bias?"

Seek Feedback: Sometimes others can see what we can't. Ask trusted friends or colleagues to point out when they think you're being biased.

Pause Before Deciding: When facing a decision, pause and consider if a bias is influencing you. It's like stopping at a crossroads to make sure you're taking the right path.

2. Developing Critical Thinking and Decision-Making Skills

Critical thinking is the art of analyzing and evaluating information without being swayed by emotions or biases. Here's how to sharpen this skill:

Question Assumptions: Don't take everything at face value. Ask questions like, "What evidence supports this?" or "Could there be another explanation?"

Consider Opposite Views: Actively seek out opinions and information that challenge your beliefs. It's like looking at both sides of a coin before deciding its value.

Decision-Making Exercises: Practice making decisions in low-stakes situations. This helps you develop a more deliberate and conscious approach to decision-making.

3. The Role of Education and Awareness

Education is a powerful tool in overcoming biases. By learning about different types of biases and how they operate, we become better equipped to recognize and counteract them.

Educational Workshops and Courses: Consider attending workshops or online courses on critical thinking and bias.

Reading and Research: Read books, articles, and research studies about biases and their effects on thinking and decision-making.

Promoting Awareness in Communities: Share your knowledge about biases with others. The more people are aware, the more we can collectively work towards minimizing their impact.

Why This Matters

By learning to overcome our biases, we not only make better decisions but also become more empathetic and understanding towards others. It opens up a world of clearer thinking, where we can see people and situations for what they truly are, rather than what our biases tell us they are.

Conclusion: Stepping Into a World of Clarity

Think of overcoming biases as stepping out of a fog into a clear day. It's not always easy, and the fog may never lift completely, but even a little bit of clarity can make a huge difference in how we perceive and interact with the world around us.

In the next chapter, we'll explore the exciting future of understanding biases, including the role of new technologies and emerging research, as we continue on our journey towards more conscious and deliberate thinking. Let's keep moving forward, towards a clearer understanding of ourselves and the world.

Chapter 8: The Future of Understanding Biases - Navigating Tomorrow's Mindscape

Embarking on a Journey to the Future of Our Minds

As we've explored the realms of biases and heuristics, it's time to look forward. What does the future hold in understanding and managing these mental tendencies? This chapter is a voyage into the emerging world of bias research and the exciting potential of technology in this domain.

Emerging Research and Theories

The study of biases is an ever-evolving field, with new insights constantly emerging. Researchers are exploring deeper into why we have biases, how they form, and the myriad ways they influence our behavior. Some of the cutting-edge areas include:

Neuroscience: Discovering how different parts of the brain contribute to bias formation.

Behavioral Economics: Understanding how biases affect economic and financial decisions.

Cultural Studies: Examining how biases vary across different cultures and societal structures.

The Role of Artificial Intelligence and Machine Learning

One of the most thrilling developments in tackling biases is the use of artificial intelligence (AI) and machine learning. These technologies have the potential to help us in ways we've never imagined:

Identifying Hidden Biases: AI can analyze vast amounts of data to uncover biases that are difficult for humans to detect.

Decision Support Systems: AI tools can provide decision-makers with unbiased data analysis, helping to counteract human biases in critical decision-making processes.

Personal Bias Checkers: Imagine an app that alerts you when you're likely being influenced by a bias. This isn't science fiction anymore; it's a real possibility with AI.

Final Thoughts on Our Unbiased Thinking Journey

As we wrap up our exploration into biases and heuristics, it's clear that the journey towards unbiased thinking is ongoing. While it's unlikely that we'll ever be completely free of biases, the future holds great promise in understanding and mitigating them.

Continuous Learning: Understanding biases is not a one-time effort; it's a continuous process of learning and self-improvement.

Community and Collaboration: Sharing insights and experiences about biases in diverse groups can lead to greater collective understanding and innovation.

Embracing Technology: Utilizing technological advancements can aid us in recognizing and countering biases more effectively.

Conclusion: A Path Toward Clarity

The future of understanding biases is not just a scientific or technological journey; it's a personal and societal one. As we move forward, armed with better tools and deeper knowledge, we can aspire to a world where decisions are made with greater clarity and fairness.

The journey towards understanding and overcoming our biases is like navigating a vast, uncharted sea. There are challenges and uncertainties, but also incredible opportunities for discovery and growth. As we continue on this journey, let's embrace both the journey and its destination – a world of clearer, more thoughtful, and unbiased thinking.

Chapter 9: Conclusion - Embracing the Journey of Mindful Awareness

Reflecting on the Path We've Traveled

As we reach the end of our exploration into the world of cognitive biases and heuristics, it's time to pause and reflect. This journey has been about more than just understanding terms and concepts; it's been about gaining insights into the workings of our own minds.

Summarizing Our Key Learnings

The Nature of Biases and Heuristics: We've discovered that cognitive biases and heuristics are like mental shortcuts – they help us navigate the complexities of life but sometimes lead us astray.

The Impact on Our Lives: From personal decisions to professional choices, biases and heuristics subtly influence our daily lives, often without us even realizing it.

Strategies for Overcoming Biases: We've explored various ways to recognize and counteract our biases – through self-awareness, critical thinking, and embracing diverse perspectives.

The Continuous Journey of Self-Awareness and Improvement

Understanding and managing our biases is not a destination; it's a continuous journey. It's about:

Constant Vigilance: Staying aware of our mental patterns and challenging them regularly.

Lifelong Learning: Continuously educating ourselves about new insights and perspectives.

Openness to Change: Being willing to adjust our thinking and behaviors as we learn and grow.

Final Reflections on the Power and Limitations of the Human Mind

Our minds are extraordinary. They have the power to create, to solve complex problems, and to connect deeply with others. Yet, they also have limitations – biases and heuristics are evidence of this. Recognizing these limitations is not a sign of weakness but a step towards greater wisdom.

Embracing the Beauty of Our Imperfect Minds

The journey through the world of biases and heuristics teaches us to embrace the beauty of our imperfect minds. It encourages us to approach life with humility, curiosity, and openness. As we continue to navigate the intricate pathways of our thoughts, let's cherish the power of our minds to change, grow, and see the world in ever-more nuanced ways.

Conclusion: A Journey Towards a Clearer Horizon

As we close this chapter, remember that every step towards understanding our biases is a step towards a clearer, more mindful existence. The journey of self-awareness and improvement is ongoing, full of challenges and opportunities. Armed with the insights we've gained, we can look forward to a future where our decisions are made with greater clarity, empathy, and wisdom. Let's keep moving forward on this journey, embracing the endless possibilities of our amazing minds.

About Freudian Trips

Welcome to Freudian Trips, your dedicated platform for diving deep into the world of psychology. We are more than just a YouTube channel or a book publisher. We are a beacon of enlightenment, making complex psychological concepts accessible and engaging for all.

Our YouTube channel is a rich repository of psychology made simple. We take the profound and often complex ideas from the world of psychology and break them down into digestible, easy-to-understand content. From the foundational theories of Freud to the cognitive insights of Piaget, we cover a broad spectrum of psychological schools and thoughts, making psychology accessible to everyone, regardless of their background or prior knowledge.

As a book publisher, we take the same approach, transforming intricate psychological theories into comprehensible narratives. Our books are not just collections of words, but vessels of wisdom that make psychology approachable and relatable. We believe that psychology should not be confined to academic circles, but should be available to all who seek to understand the human mind and behavior.

At Freudian Trips, we believe in the power of curiosity and the pursuit of knowledge. We are here to stoke the fires of your curiosity, to guide you on your intellectual journey, and to help you navigate the fascinating world of psychology.

If you are someone who is not afraid to question, to explore, and to learn, then you are in the right place. Join us on this journey of exploration, as we make psychology easy to understand, one concept at a time.

Be sure to visit our Youtube channel at: www.freudiantrips.com/youtube

You can also visit us on the web at www.freudiantrips.com

Welcome to The Freudian Trip community. Stay curious. Stay enlightened.